Making Comic Books

Text by Michael Teitelbaum
Comic art by Howard Bender and David Tanguay

The Child's World®
www.childsworld.com

Published in the United States of America by The Child's World®
P.O. Box 326 • Chanhassen, MN 55317-0326
800-599-READ • www.childsworld.com

For Wally Green and Paul Kuhn, who taught me how to bring a
story to life on the comic-book page.—M. T.

ACKNOWLEDGMENTS

The Child's World®: Mary Berendes, Publishing Director

Produced by Shoreline Publishing Group LLC
President / Editorial Director: James Buckley, Jr.
Designer: Tom Carling, carlingdesign.com
Cover Art: Slimfilms
Copy Editor: Beth Adelman

Illustration Credits
All comic art created by Howard Bender and David Tanguay.

Photo Credits
Interior—Corbis: 7; courtesy of the subjects: 9, 13, 21;
Photos.com: 16; Shoreline Publishing: 29

LIBRARY OF CONGRESS CATALOGING-IN-PUBLICATION DATA

Teitelbaum, Michael.
  Making comic books / by Michael Teitelbaum ; artwork by
Howard Bender ; additional artwork by David Tanguay.
    p. cm. — (Boys rock!)
  Includes bibliographical references and index.
  ISBN 1-59296-733-7 (library bound : alk. paper)
  1. Comic books, strips, etc.—Publishing—Juvenile literature.
  2. Comic books, strips, etc.—Authorship—Juvenile literature.
  I. Bender, Howard. II. Title. III. Series.
  PN6710.T45 2006
  741.5—dc22
                        2006001636

CONTENTS

Beginnings

An evil alien threatens an entire city. A superhero flashes across the comic-book page. Will the hero arrive in time? Will the city be saved from disaster? Month after month, comic books tell exciting stories just like this.

But how did that comic book come to be? In this book, you'll find out. Follow along to see how our comic—starring Pulsar and the Protector—was created.

Comic books are the work of a team of creative and talented people. The person in charge of the team is the **editor**. The editor makes sure everything is done on time and looks over the comic book at every stage.

A comic book begins with a meeting between the editor and the writer. Together they discuss ideas for the story and answer a lot of important questions, such as "Which characters will be used?" and "What will the **setting** be?"

One of the editor's jobs is to check all the words to make sure they are spelled correctly. The editor also makes sure each character has the same powers from one book to the next.

Once those questions are answered, the writer can get to work. It takes imagination to decide how the characters will get into— and out of—trouble.

The First Comic Books

Comic strips have appeared in newspapers since the 1800s. The first comic books came out in the early 1930s. They were just collections of the newspaper strips. By the late 1930s, original comic-book stories were being created. Many of those first stories were about superheroes.

Before any pictures are drawn for a comic book, the writer must write a **script**. The comic-book script is the guide from which the whole book will be put together.

"Script" can also mean the written-out copy of all the words the actors will say in a movie or TV show.

In the script, the writer breaks the story into pages. Then the writer breaks each page into boxes called **panels**. Our comic on page 5 has three panels.

Within each panel, the writer first tells the artist which characters, action, and setting to draw.

Then the writer decides what the characters will say. These words are called the **dialogue** (DY-uh-log). The writer also chooses whether there will be sound effects in that panel.

The script next goes to a special kind of artist called a **penciler**. The penciler (Howard Bender, in this case) creates a rough drawing using a pencil. He decides how big the panels will be and how to show in pictures what the writer described with words.

OPPOSITE PAGE
Compare this drawing with the finished art on page 5.

In this rough stage (seen on page 11), the penciler isn't worried about getting everything perfect. Howard just wants to see how the characters and backgrounds will fit together on the page.

11

COMING Alive

The next stage, known as "pencils," is where the penciler really brings the story to life. Here, Howard adds details to the characters. They are given **facial expressions** and full costumes. The backgrounds are filled out, too. The artist gives the reader a clearer idea of what the characters are doing and feeling and where the action is taking place.

Artist Howard Bender, who drew our comic-book page, works in his studio. Howard has drawn comic books for both Marvel and DC Comics.

Tools of the Trade

Different types of pencils draw different kinds of lines. The lines create different looks and feelings in a drawing. A hard, sharp pencil gives a thin line, which is good for adding details. A thicker pencil is used for shading.

The penciler draws the "real" parts of the picture, such as people, trees, and buildings. He must also use his imagination to create some parts. For instance, the energy bursts coming from Pulsar's weapon were created using only Howard's imagination and skill.

OPPOSITE PAGE

Compare these pencils with the rough drawing on page 11 and with the finished comic-book page on page 5.

Look at the facial expressions of Pulsar and the Protector in the pencils. Compare them to the way the faces were drawn on page 11 to see how much detail has been added.

When the pencils are finished, they are checked over by the editor. Then they are ready to go to an artist called an **inker**.

Pencil lines aren't dark enough or strong enough to be printed in the final comic book. So an inker must go over the pencil lines with black ink. Sometimes the same artist does both the pencils and the inks (as Howard has done).

At other times, one artist does the pencils and another does the inks.

Inkers use special pens with different tips, called **nibs**. Different nibs produce different types of lines. Thin lines are used for outlines and details. Thicker lines are used for shading and mood. A great inker can really make comic-book art come alive.

See how the ink has made the pencil lines bolder and stronger?

The inks are also used to add shadows. By using lines of different thickness, the inker can make the characters pop out of the background. The inks help give **two-dimensional** artwork a **three-dimensional** feel.

The inker also fills in some areas of the art completely, making them totally black. For example, the inker has filled in most of Pulsar's costume, making the character seem more dangerous than he did in the pencils.

OPPOSITE PAGE

Compare these inks with the pencils on page 15, the rough drawing on page 11, and the finished comic-book page on page 5.

FINAL Steps

The finished inks are exciting, but one more step is needed to bring the comic page to life—color! The artist who chooses and adds color to the black-and-white artwork is called a **colorist**. For years, comic-book coloring was done with markers and special colored inks. They were painted onto the black-and-white page. These days, colorists work on computers.

Here's David Tanguay at work coloring the Protector page that appears in this book.

Using his artistic and computer skills, colorist David Tanguay can turn a piece of black-and-white art into a full-color painting.

One of the most important parts of the colorist's work deals with light.

A character's costume must be the same color in every panel and on every page. But that doesn't mean that the characters look exactly the same every time you see them. The colorist must imagine how the lighting should be in each panel. Should it be bright and sunny? Should it be dark and stormy? The lighting will change how the character looks in each scene.

OPPOSITE PAGE
Compare this fully colored section with the inks on page 19, the pencils on page 15, the rough drawing on page 11, and the finished comic-book page on page 5.

By looking at the inks, you can't really tell what time of day our scene is taking place. But by adding the sunset in the first panel, the colorist lets you know that the battle between Pulsar and the Protector is taking place in the late afternoon.

Now the page is drawn and colored. But what about the words?

Putting words onto the artwork is the job of the **letterer**. For the Protector page, colorist David Tanguay was also the letterer. First, he created a title for the story (above). For this, he used big, bold letters.

He also placed the **captions**, which are words in a square or rectangular box.

MES PULSAR!

THE PROTECTOR, SWORN DEFENDER OF EARTH, BATTLES HIS GREATEST FOE, THE ALIEN KNOWN AS *PULSAR!*

Captions aren't spoken or thought by any character. They set the scene or lead the reader into the action.

In the past, comic-book lettering was done by hand. The letterer would write the words right onto the pencils before the page was inked. These days, the lettering is done on a computer.

Bold, bright colors are often used for the headlines. Look for smaller caption boxes to find out more about the setting of a comic-book scene.

Speech Balloons

> IF PULSAR'S ENERGY BURSTS STRIKE THAT DAM, THE *WHOLE CITY* BELOW WILL BE *FLOODED!*

> *!.* NEVER STOP *ROTECTOR!*

A speech balloon has a smooth line around it and a pointy tail leading to the character, like the one shown here. This means the character is saying the words aloud. A wavy line around the balloon usually means it shows what the character is thinking.

After the captions, the letterer adds the dialogue. Remember, the dialogue is the words that characters are saying or thinking. The dialogue is placed into speech balloons. Often the letterer has to be very creative to find space for all the balloons.

Finally, the letterer adds the sound effects. These words represent sounds made by energy bursts, explosions, or other noises. They help make the story come to life.

Our comic page is almost done. There's just one more step before you can bring it home and read it!

Sound Effects

What does it sound like when Pulsar fires an energy burst, or when the Protector's force shield blocks the burst? The sound effects let you know. They help make the comic-book story seem more like a movie.

Have you been following all the steps? The writer wrote the script. The penciler turned those words into pictures. The inker brought depth and shadows to the artwork. The colorist turned the black-and-white page into full color. The letterer added the words. Now it's time for the final step.

The computer files containing the artwork are made into metal or plastic sheets called **plates**. Then these plates are put onto a printing press.

How long does it all take? From the first meeting with the writer to the finished comic book's arrival in stores, it can take three or four months!

The plates are covered with ink and pressed against paper to print the image. The paper is put together into a comic book. Finally, the printed comic book is shipped to a store near you!

The hard work of all the people on the comic-book team pays off when a kid gets to read their work!

GLOSSARY

captions   words in rectangular boxes that tell you what is happening in a scene

colorist   the artist who adds color to a black-and-white comic drawing

dialogue   what characters say or think

editor   the person in charge of all the creative people who work on a comic book

facial expressions   how a person changes their face to show what they are feeling

inker   the artist who goes over the pencils with ink

letterer   the person who puts the words onto a comic page

nibs   different pen points used for inking

panels   boxes on a comic page that contain artwork

penciler   the artist who first draws the comic art, using a pencil

plates   metal or plastic sheets covered with ink that are used to print the actual comic-book pages

script   in a comic book, the guide from which each page will be built

setting   the location where the action takes place

three-dimensional   a solid object that has three dimensions—height, width, and depth

two-dimensional   a flat image that has just two dimensions—height and width

FIND OUT MORE

BOOKS

The Art of Making Comic Books
by Michael Morgan Pellowski and Howard Bender
(Lerner Publications, Minneapolis, MN) 1995
Our own penciler gives tips on becoming an artist.

Creating the X-Men: How Comic Books Come to Life
by James Buckley, Jr.
(Dorling Kindersley, New York) 2000
Marvel Comics experts take you behind the scenes of one of
the most popular comic-book teams.

The DC Comics Guide to Penciling Comics
by Klaus Jansen
(Watson-Guptill Publications, New York) 2002
One of the major comic-book companies reveals its secrets.

How to Draw Comics the Marvel Way
by Stan Lee and John Buscema
(Fireside, New York) 1984
Step-by-step instructions on drawing famous heroes.

WEB SITES

Visit our home page for lots of links about making comic books:
www.childsworld.com/links

Note to Parents, Teachers, and Librarians: We routinely check our Web links to
make sure they're safe, active sites—so encourage your readers to check them out!

INDEX

MICHAEL TEITELBAUM has been a writer, editor, and producer of children's books, comic-books, and magazines for more than 25 years. Michael has written books based on comic-book characters such as Superman, Batman, Spider-Man, and Garfield. He also created and edited *Spider-Man Magazine*. Michael and his wife, Sheleigh, split their time between New York City and their farmhouse in the Catskill Mountains of upstate New York.